W0115769

A Visit to Civilization

WESLEYAN POETRY

A Visit to

Civilization

Sandra McPherson

Wesleyan University Press
MIDDLETOWN, CONNECTICUT

Published by Wesleyan University Press, Middletown, CT 06459
© 2002 by Sandra McPherson
Printed in the United States of America

5 4 3 2 1

.

LIBRARY OF CONGRESS CATALOGING-IN-PUBLICATION DATA
A visit to civilization / Sandra McPherson.
   p. cm.   (Wesleyan poetry)
ISBN 0–8195–6518–0 (alk. paper) — ISBN 0–8195–6519–9 (pbk. : alk. paper)
   I. Title.
PS3563.A326 V67 2002
811'.54—dc21   2001005384

My husband Walter Pavlich continues to take me to visit civilization . . . daily.
This volume is dedicated to him.

ACKNOWLEDGMENTS

Grateful acknowledgment is made to the journals and publications in which many of
these poems first appeared: *The Yale Review, Field, Poetry, The Southern Review,
The Paris Review, The Progressive* (409 E. Main Street, Madison, WI 53703 © 1997),
*Plough-shares, The Missouri Review, TriQuarterly, Redstart, ZYZZYVA, Double-
Take, Massachusetts Review, The Kenyon Review, Manoa, The Iowa Review, Western
Humanities Review, Poetry Ireland Review, The American Voice, Oxymoron* (www.
oxymoron.com), *Obsidian, The Agni Review,* and *Metre* (Dublin).

"The Walls an Interview" first appeared in TriQuarterly, a publication of Northwest-
ern University. "Peppertree and Tea" first appeared in Mañoa: A Pacific Journal of
International Writing in summer 1997 (vol. 9:1), published by the University of
Hawai'i Press. "A Vigil 2 AM, County Jail" and "In Her Image" originally appeared in
Ploughshares (vol 25:1).

"What's in My Journal" copyright 1991, 1998 by the estate of William Stafford.
Reprinted from *The Way It Is: New & Selected Poems* with the permission of Gray-
wolf Press, Saint Paul, Minnesota.

The University of California at Davis aided considerably with several faculty research
grants.

Contents

I

To a Penny Postcard, © 1911

A woman's interested head, long sprigs of green,
and a loose, supple ribbon the blush
pink of the rose shaded by my apple tree
sashes it all.

> *What*
> *do we live for,*
> *if it is not*
> *to make Life*
> *less difficult*
> *for one another.*

Not one of the pharmacy cure-alls from its day:
They usually use the word "easy."

And who doesn't know many
who would answer the rhetorical query,
No, for me. Or no one else will.

Very pretty, the sprigs and the satin of the loopy bowknot
and the font where we find difficulty.
And rather intrepid, the look in the woman's eyes.
She probes the words at an angle;
her hair, full and clean, as if it could polish them.

She lived
but it's a long time since a penny.
I don't wonder how she lived.
We know, don't we?

Isn't life easier for us,
being sent this postcard
from a bygone mailbox
and a vanished heart—
yes, even extinct it makes life
less troublesome for me,
not quite lost each day. And pretty.

The Stranger Melody

The stranger, Melody,
who in early spring

felt among the weeds I brought in
to the consignment shop a full silk blouse

of a deep mimeograph color
and wished aloud to buy it—

next week, when she'd have the money—
has come now with her money

to make it hers. It is the day
the chlorine-pale flowers of the Norway maple

fall in a limelight around their pedestal,
drop a bouquet garni atop Melody's black car.

When we talk—"I'm not
the harpist I would like to be," she says,

and leaning forward in the purple pleats
goes on to pry advice from me

as a mother—
How can she free her only son

to risk himself?
"He does it now

—he crosses the street; he hides from me till dark—
but guiltily," as she keeps after him

with plucking calls. Then "Why
did I do it, Mother," he confesses,

burying his face in her blouse-folds.
"In this very shirt you're selling me," she points,
"He will, you know,"

squaring her shoulders, envying her own body,
this welling after-dark raiment

passed from my life,
"unless I do something

about myself very soon," she says,
threading away from my door,

pausing before the floral footlights
until she steps around them,

crushing none.

Trading

Phyllis says she makes a good bear.
I don't really want to trade a quilt
for a teddy bear. Neither
do I want Phyllis feeling bad.

Phyllis wants a quilt I own
stuffed with lace curtains and underwear.
She wants it for her young son's bed. Oh,
I do not know anymore—

souls have sunk deep and found no furnishings there:
Even of guilt
the purest place is absolutely bare.
Phyllis wants something she can make

into a pillow for her boutique.
She'd rather trade than sell.
I live at the bottom of a well,
must keep everything just so

and keep it all.
Swap me something with butterflies on it.
We have to trade what gives me
pain for what gives you cheer.

Something the needle has touched
prickles for each of us.
I want to give, reach the top shelf and thrust toward
Phyllis a thing to redefine

as satisfactory
that had no worth before,
just its own empty body,
its bare-faced history,

that as it changes hands
is changing
perfectly—
ugly to beautiful.

A Gentlewoman

"I couldn't *yearn*," she marveled.
Before marriage, with a nervous edge
she'd written poems that her teacher praised.
They excited and needed her; she made them
burn and be. But ever since the ceremony,
they had stayed away. She saw herself so changed
by love, the page waved off her wedded ink.
Maybe it stayed, that way, truest. Stanzas abandoned
the elegant young bride because she couldn't yearn,
she said.

   "I am *seething* with ideas," she breathes
and looks across the flitting birds and blowing herbs
of the courtyard toward the locked door
of her studio, her wheel, her tiles, her paints,
her remembered subjects, objects that she poses.
She supposes she'll quit cooking. But she grieves
her works are never fully realized. She knows
art, has collected figures gripping figures galloping,
trees that blaze in red and sagey open spaces,
bezels and cants of hills, stipples and stains
of seasons. Hands of geniuses tremble
her walls, and her will. In widowhood
she's back at her source, though frail
in her cashmere dressing gown and wing-
shaped diamond brooch. She leans forward,
stressing, "I am just seething with ideas."

Brokenness: A Month's Diary

Multiple Sclerosis

On the last day of the wildness workshop
Kay and Jimmy stood Kay's photographs
on chairs around the room
and hearing me admire them said, "Choose one."
Because I want something from each phase of hers,
I picked the newest, with its ancient look:
She's been working with broken pots.
Kay described how some arrangements
of broken pots are just a jumble of debris
but very rarely one heap shifts
into something fuller than its parts,
as with this new "Cavewoman"
and her earlier "Broken Rice Bowl and Chrysanthemum."
(Mountains are looking in the workshop window.)
Her groupings are a personal compact
with fractured things—what medicine
can't do as well. I was tempting dementia
to dwell for years on quilts' basis in the broken,
in re-use of croppings of wholeness.
But Kay's work is re-use. And it leads to interiors,
new planes revealed by the breakage.

Where this ridge scales off into the lake,
Captain Richards on his research ship
shows us how lowering the Secchi Disc
we can measure exactly where,
in the thistle-cobalt Tahoe water,
a body goes unclear.
Raise the plate till it reappears,
then reckon the site of clarity.
Average the extremes: You have
an audit of transparency.

While the Secchi Disc is unbreakable plastic—
a simple tool, so nothing can go wrong—
the original device of estimation
was a scientist's wife's china dinner plate.
(The lake's eyes swim all around the plate.)

Women and damage. Broken men.
Jimmy and Kay have a working method
for pulling things together. Today
they are photographing me: "Think of
yourself only as a device to reflect the light."
They use a gray card, specially for this rim
of the continent, to measure "average light."
Then, how to look to give that light some wit?
Kay says, "You look at the lens as you would breathe
into a horse's nostril."
(The horses are breathing all around us.)
Jimmy sets up all the equipment, adjusts distances,
matches light meter readings with film speed,
rehearses a frame, then yields
the chance to press the cable release.
He moves away and Kay
concenters behind the camera,
differs, breaks into his run-through,
reframes vertically (because she says she knows
"how hard it is to stand"), and she

takes *her* picture.
She shows me the box of havoc
she used in the photograph I chose.
The relics take me by surprise:
The color they're in diminishes them.
And none of the gleam is in the eyes and mouth
that Kay maneuvered into them.
Kay made the ruins people and rocks,
people coming and going among ruins,
in an eroding world.
That pot was smashed by wild little girls.

I think of Kay following the military doctor's orders
to sleep with a glass test tube
up her vagina to stretch it out.
Did he believe she wouldn't bend or break?
How could he fix a shattered Vet? But fresh

chrysanthemums and a cracked-open rice bowl:
they're tact. Kay said, "I lovingly held
each piece and asked, 'What goes *with* it?'
The brokenness gave it freedom."
She let chrysanthemum petals complete
the missing rim of the bowl. "It escaped,"
she said, "into its own wholeness."
(The bowl is all around us, watching.)
Kay answers when I outright ask
what fractions or integrities
she would like for creations, "I can use
saints, I can use holy objects,
send me battered shells or stones or wood,
send me any small box, flowers real or realistically
fake, send me anything that breaks."

From the great fusion of sea water,
I am collecting, for Kay, what's left
of sand dollars, scallops, mussel hulls, to play
patina games with dull opacity and shining.
Behind the beach, combing a trail with small
pourings of sun barely reaching the forest floor,
lighting a fern or two, Walter says,
"Spotlights of sun in broken unison."
In town, four retarded men
wander, with me, a gallery
of oil duplicates of water scenery.
Large seascapes lit from within
surround the quiet slowness of the men.
Their group coheres.
Through the second story door comes the sea roar.
The wind rolls gingerly around in there.

Every painted wave breaks at eye level.
(The gray drum skin of storm skies,
storm skin, wraps around us.)

And then, outside, a thing that must be whole:
floating up from the south, a blimp—
over ocean swells, just past the craggy outcrop.
Everything, water, sky, and blimp,
wears silver, gray, and white.
Photographers (and glassblowers)
must love this. —And then,
I hear from Kay at last. She says
of the two rolls she took of me
only the eyes came out. I grant
I reflect funny, maybe incoherently.
Her louvered proof
auditions my echelons of ash.

If I could send Kay a saint,
saints "take" better than I in black and white,
though in the book I rest with to end this
full day emptying into reservations
I've made for the next,
saints too are at the end of their use
and out of print:

> *Fragments of images*
> *were sometimes removed*
> *and thrown into a field*
> *as offering for abundant harvest.*
> *Or parts of images burned,*
> *the ashes used*
> *for Ash Wednesday.*
> *Or engaged as relics.*
> *An image broken*
> *or damaged beyond repair*
> *would be utterly incinerated*

and its cinders gathered
for the purposes mentioned.

Beyond repair, I begin to gather purposes.
My friends will know how best to choose one.

In Her Image

French postcard, circa World War I

In agreeing to be the crucified woman,
she knew she would need to hang there
with no pockets, no purse, no pearls.
She would know how to stretch into it
when the time came. Did she enjoy
an innate ballerina who could express
befitting grace? While still her bearing
should look disciplinary, chastening.
Express duress. She must suffer
while blooming with a boast of pulchritude
the lighting director could work with.
At the tryouts, the rest of us were already
too mangled with practice nails, and slivers.

She stepped right up, and now she is *holding* on.
Jesus as evangelist from girlhood, a young savant
known for finespun sayings and secrecy
revealed as sorrow. Her death would fall
somewhere in her menstrual cycle.
Her belly invites most—soft and so
slightly split into those two lobes
which make apricots and peaches
superior to the moon. Lustrous,
a stage-curtain rope knots right over
pubic hair. Feet bound with ribbon,
a satin tether to appeal to some, she
ails ungaunt, her edges sled-round,
cambered. Coifed in the same style
as her carnality: in even waves, marcelled.

Are agony's good looks art's job,
or labor's contract, or sex's by swoon?
Whatever, they're hers. And the age's.
Real senselessness, stupefying power
over lives, eventually tore men's
faces off. Their leaders made millions
rot millions. Many choked on rats' mud.
Flies had no teeth for skulls
so there it stopped. What did this have to do
with our sacrificing, sacrificing our breasts
barely between a triangle of bleeding nails?
How we numbed evil. How unbearable
we made goodness feel.

Six Movements for Portraits of Erzulie

spirit flags, sewn in Haiti, 1990

Two images of love: one, a child artisan's, abstract,
with antennae, feelers; the other, something a child
couldn't make—

sharp swords to the heart.

The child's swords float loose, exterior, aim toward earth—

crutches that don't reach.

Vapors from a rum cup. Flash from rectangular goat's eyes.

Child's goddess of love. Adults' salty deity.

In the child's, the heart is the face.

When the initiate rolls awake on the bed in her sanctuary,
goose quills working through the pillow
scratch her eyelids and cheeks. Erzulie looks
brokenhearted, sinister.
As the boy sewed on her fingernails
(each a sole clear sequin
fixed with a glass bead,
the same as tears only
tears are pinker and more drawn out,
thinner in the calipers)
he glittered.

Who gores her heart seven times?
I think she does, working the cutlery in
as one inserts thermometers to cook,
then folding her hands crisply away, blood
on her cuffs.
Oh that color—of blood rinsed
from a man's shaving sink.
Never far from her hand,
busy gold hilts collect no dust.

Pleasurable, promiscuous, passionate—
the heart that doesn't know
how to be a widow.

But sunset reflecting in the face
shows otherwise—there's a scowl
to sensuality.

When the heart and the face are separate,
you have to keep your eye on both.
Modestly, the flame of love's candle blows to the side.
It is never clear and pure, never straight ascension.
And it's not because we're breathing on it
that it slants away.
Flame has to be our sloping, dwindling mirror,
our exact wax features
burning up.

Maybe you think it makes a difference
how she is expressed: as a heated human figure
or, vaguer, as pigment and power.
What kind of portrait did you go to bed with,
wive, cheat on, and miss as a symbol
of your promising years?

And for women it is the same:
She is the idea
that beauty is rich, love poor and bare,
she is thinking that way,
trying to get out of
the single life of doctrine.

Finally she leaves you.
Only her abstraction is coming home.

NOTE: Erzulie (sometimes spelled Ezili) is the Haitian deity of beauty, luxury, and
love. "Coquettish, sensual, pleasure-loving and extravagant" (Metraux), she derives
from the Yoruba goddess Oshun and is also a version of Our Lady of Sorrows.

Design of Days

According to a short forehand passage in her diary it's Sunday morning.
The husband packs decoys, will leave for hunting in an hour,
be in the blind two days. She looks forward to learning
why she calms down, reduces power,
gets along on a less lethal current.
She'll watch intensely, discover the new design
of her days. What will go differently?
Thinks she could sketch the white pine,
the unusual coastal snow muffling the waves.
For the present it is enough to read Buson,
his series of verses in the persona
of a woman traveling the same road as he.
"Fucking snow," the hunter says. It coats his road.
She gentles him, veiling for herself
how frightening it will be, in time,
for him to know, for her to see him recognize,
which man's voice she craves.

Four Anonymous Women with Bright Sad Mouths

$7. Hand-colored. All wearing the same pendant.
Jade, jade, jade, and jade.
Filipinas? Malay? Silk and rayon
best clothes. Sisters. But it is
their bright red unhappy mouths I see first.
Bright unhappiness.

Ray's is an open barn with a radiating wood stove in its center. I
bought the picture directly from big rough Ray, who bought it off
someone else for how little? And he made what—$5—from me. He
saw something in it.

Layers of dust from the Gravenstein Highway.
A history of moisture
eating oyster crackers of paint off the frame.
But print fabrics still glad, and glad
their beautician-scrolled hair.
The formal photographer worked them
into a diamond conformation, they're its bright corners,
points of a family gem.

You cannot tell exactly what has been abandoned
by their identical rejectable mouths.
Words, curses, held in common by that quartet of expressions,
the red slots, penny arcade, parking meter, slot
machine, cat cry, ringworm,
red toy race track, mouths.

A woman dementia-convinced, in her wavery dimension, thinks
she is abandoned, leans around the corner where her kind husband
left her to save her long slow walking to the restaurant. She looks as
forsaken as a wild clattering deer wandered onto asphalt. In some
intersections no love intersects.

I used to watch the nudists in a Santa Barbara canyon
wave us—girls and students—off, want
their privacy yet want the sun,
that large a share of radiance.
I offered to be like the sun, that approving.
They taught me to learn
further plainness.

God wove the fabric of the beetle's skin.
Or someone else might think *forged* it.
The beetle god is a blacksmith
with a loom.

"Suffering must be anonymous"—half-caught narration to a film on Mexico. *Penitentes* in black cloth head-masks and robes, "Custom demands that suffering be anonymous."

The old nudists felt politically oppressed. The greatest original tango composer was persecuted for changing form. Who, really, wants to be remembered as the heavy hand against nudists and tangoists? As their tormentor? As someone who would wear them down, proscribe them?

Disillusionment.
Their mouths are an earlier stage of it.
It reaches greatness in tango.

The pessimistic and the disillusioned were much admired—one singer "famous for the line, 'The 20th Century is a trash heap. No one can deny it . . .'"—for giving a mouth to zero.

All suffering must be anonymous, the narrator said, and costumed.

We decide not to go near the cliff
this time, the most worn risked path,
children too go there,
field trips to the edge.
Looking on, the wild iris.
Then I remember the blindness of plants . . .

That's a rafflesia on her dress, the largest flower. I recall it from research on largest and smallest plants, caught in the middle as we are. Her gray suited sister, equal.

A flower, if you blink, from bowel to breast. Proportionally, imagine the lonely room, the abandoner's missing heart from ceiling to floor.

In the evening the mists drape . . .
just exist and nothing else does.
The strong earthline lifts
a full coastline of fog.
The harbor lights, in pecking order
or as if pets of light graduating
one by one from training school—
over the baylands
the harbor lights come on.
The egrets preview another pond.

Where else would rafflesia appear on daily wear? Fourteen species from Malaya & the East Indies, of which the enormous red- and cream-flowered Sumatran *R. arnoldii* is well known from models of it seen in museums. "Species are impossible to identify by their superficial resemblances, since it is the *structures inside the flowers* that distinguish them." Anonymity, but not inside.

All their mouths are open, teeth, worry, concern.

You think you know lifting.
The fog—too much for humans—
waterweight miles broad—
wet baggage, soaked work . . .
Everything wet begs. Oblige.
Give out of pocket, the purse of every cell.

In one antiques shop in the old superseded capital on the bay,
between refineries and mothball fleet,
tins of Elgin second hands—
what does it mean they didn't work
throughout the wars? lay still through peace?

Muteness is healing, they said, when I lost my voice.
Muteness keeps all concepts in solution,
casting out none.
Speech seems an outcast, a bit *stray*.

In Guerneville the slim men and large women without garments
glowed fully in the sun around the pool. I walked down in the
evening, slipped off my dress, swam with the shapes. My shape wel-
comed me. I'm still slow from an anesthetic. But I don't have to
speak and make sense underwater. The women embrace in the pool.
Tall old bay trees and redwoods watch the bathers wash away the
persecution.

"I can hardly believe a nudist could ever attempt to take his or
her life; it seems to me unthinkable—a nudist is an optimist to the
extreme degree above everything else."

The women's lipstick hurts to see
but seems not punitive
toward the source of their care.
Under the magnifying glass I see
the forward sister's chained jade
is only painted on by the touch-up artist.
She has no ornament.

I picture them standing side by side in bathing suits, watching a
river . . .

NOTE: The quote in the third stanza from the end derives from *Sunshine & Health*,
June 1948.

II

ᚺᚺᚺᚺᚺᚺᚺᚺᚺᚺᚺᚺᚺᚺᚺᚺᚺᚺᚺᚺᚺᚺᚺᚺ

What's in My Journal

Odd things, like a button drawer. Mean
things, fishhooks, barbs in your hand.
But marbles too. A genius for being agreeable.
Junkyard crucifixes, voluptuous
discards. Space for knickknacks, and for
Alaska. Evidence to hang me, or to beatify.
Clues that lead nowhere, that never connected
anyway. Deliberate obfuscation, the kind
that takes genius. Chasms in character.
Loud omissions. Mornings that yawn above
a new grave. Pages you know exist
but you can't find them. Someone's terribly
inevitable life story, maybe mine.
      —William Stafford

WHAT YOU MAKE CAN PREVENT THIS

      —WWII American propaganda poster, featuring an eye-level
         white cross topped with a helmet and stuck in beach sand in
         the South Pacific

Diary with Fishhooks

George W. Grow, Northeastern Pennsylvania, 1876-1880

My own words, no two
lists alike, rosters
of what you owe
on goods edible, drapeable,
hammerable, accounts
payable.
You know me,
my name is Grow.

A large fishhook sunk through October
emerges timeworked pages later
among the celebratory year's eclipses,
two suns, two moons.
Every few days a further barb—
a lock on the stream of the diary—
anchors the writer in keen seclusion.
They more than do for paper clips.
Wounded, we whine
(but why should we?)
of finding no prized secrets.
He lives, labors, balances
where people keep up
on each other, where accounts
and not confessions, worths
not sins, are tallied in patience
until settled and signed off.
Cloistered or caught?—the wriggling
purchases: potash, shoes, lemons
and coffee, maple sugar and shirting,
bushels of potatoes, nails, hinges,
bushels of oats, a bar of soap,
vest buttons, shoe buttons,

21 pounds pork, 3 yards gingham,
butter and the wife's expensive hat,
tin pail, belt strings, and beans.
Here, lying in wait, tied flies on hooks,
one with unfaded red hair,
a fox's or a wiry child's
reared now, now sleep's.
Hook through the combs
of his bee garden, his horn of smoke.
Through flow and slow overflow
of honey . . .
              Trim to go on
Anny Strowbridge Coffin. Poor fish, *the man*
that drowned last Monday was found today.
Uncovered with a stab.
Hidden behind this peril, his order
for a dozen Sunday School songbooks.
Secreted under others, all the weeks
he fashioned his skiff and its oars.
He never says what he loves
or what he shuns, just what he does.
Impaled, verses of Paul, Matthew, John,
the temperance meeting and the Centennial train
riding the excursion of our history.
Snagged for a hundred years
until I release them—pages of
dinner squirrels and sawn board feet;
gaffed on the backward tine
until it releases me—
these nosing fingertips.
The probe is patchable,
the quest not harmed.
Leader with dried river running it
curled up in this creel of time spent
stairs-building and church-painting,
bringing provision to the handmade table.
Pierced, with an original idea,

no office boy he,
George Grow, thorny for privacy.

> *Of course: They're*
> *my own words. I set them true*
> *on this new patented page surface*
> *erasable with dew*
> *or spangle off a well's bucket.*
> *Some are God's own words:*
> *"And Jesus when he was baptized*
> *went up straight out of the water . . ."*
> *Remove a fishhook to continue.*
> *I launched the boat.*
> *Long ago for breakfast*
> *there were trout.*

Toy Soldier

circa 1930

With the ethereal radio man,
his spinning wheel of fine wire,
and with the disheveled wounded,
who are legion, child, you play,
but your favorite is the warrior
whose hand is raised to smite
this gong with whatever
that musical utensil is called,
that weapon against gongs
that makes metal suffer
great shudders of urgent tone.
They swamp the jittery lull.
And see: As it would *not* be
in the symphony, the instrument
is shingled "Gas Alarm."

And when, child, you make
believe, the small gong swinging
in the current of your breath,
you imagine the performance,
whole round quavers ebbing,
and you know you should
envision the strangling mist.
But why, when you're safe?
The soldier hasn't struck it yet.
His mask's filtering eyes
match battered tin camp cups,
let him search the mud-green
blasted battle map, sigh in
no toxin. Toxin, tocsin,
you play with the names.

He is no toy Tchaikovsky,
but a child cannot know that yet.
The instant the alarmist's
duty becomes music,
it re-composes the world.
Except it save someone,
a whole symphony's
worth of men,
it sings without the slightest
resonance of the sublime.
Is there no sorrow with a toy?
Eventually there is,
but it may take year upon year
to reach that threshold
when the child amused
into manhood will volunteer.

Specialty

With the uninvited need to draw
the human body, he was conversant,
for he bought and sold estates
of those who drew it privately then died.

His guests, collectors of such an artist, arrived
out of the public world, their eyes
lowered from the sharp edifice of city sun.
It hurt the way it cut corners of stone.

He held ready the photograph
from their wedding announcement
and compared the steady image of the groom
with the real man in several motions

of the head, glance down, gaze up
to the more flushed true skin
(the photo from winter shows him dispositioned
on a rainy radius of evergreens).

A pretty good likeness
he hadn't, before this facing,
been able to set ticking with heartbeat
or murmur, off the beat.

His original patron and friend, the bride,
stirred about his loft. He turned to her:
Even the cartoons were sexy,
didn't she think? Sketched in the thirties,

with—in the line—workman's labor
to be . . . not racy but racy enough.
"Not naughty and not nice. Just him,"
he says of the artist. In one, a stripper

walks naked, wan, for the first time
in front of the guys
who roil behind a little orchestra
shivering at her feet,

her tippy (like hardening
stems on two downed maple leaves) high heels.
She's freezing with stage fright.
Her shoulders squeeze together.

If flesh, she would be a very old woman now,
but surely she'd remember that first undressing.
He points to another aspiringly
libertine work, a deepening

oil, of a nickelodeon—
one way or another the lights go out
and you have this recollection
burning ahead of you

of a drawable body.
Make an initial contour.
And don't miss the gawking men's girlfriends'
faces at the burlesque, how they look carefully

expressionless. The host notices
every finespun detail, bend and crescent.
This practice of his, a client can see, whets real love,
exposed love, every particular saved into feeling.

The debuting stripper,
though not yet up to her full savor,
throws no protective shadow over her shyness.
As the couple scan her

in the home of her frame
and choose to take her home—
pull the thread of her ink line out through
the keyhole eye of afternoon—

the dealer shakes the husband's
real, round, and roseate hand
and kisses the wife in caricature
good-bye.

Approaching Robert Hayden

Of men remembered in the Capitol, who is marble, who
Is bronze? I know Fulton gets to sit
To monkey with his mockup steamboat. A traffic
Of pedestals, a history all elbows.

Or all transport: great early airplanes—
Belief in the flight of hooped costumes, baleened corsets—
Are leashed to a ceiling and buoyed up by a citizenry
Breathing. Outside the Carter White House

The screech of a loudspeaking hawk
Frightens starlings into using their airpower.
And there's a man visiting inside whose choices move me
I'd like to compliment—but I delay

The President in a handshake more easily
Than brag admiration to a blind stranger.
At breakfast there's a second chance: he sits
Hearing the fountain, warming the plants

And reading the *Post* or, rather, rubbing it
Across his glasses. Words are camouflaged in his eyes.
But bother him? And so I don't, I speak
To B. J. Lofty and his white Chrysler cab:

"To the sculpture garden."
I go my January way; it's the start
Of a decade, Balzac wears seven veils
Of snow, Hayden moves into his marble shack.

[1980]

37

The Thorn-Shaver on Fifth

Falling to
his potting-mix-brown
avenue—
particular thorns—
each sliced
to an urbane demise

for a rose.
The florist's apprentice,
who might have made
a whittler in the woods,
supposes they perspire
under each spine

and finds the work worth
sitting on
the points of his bones.
On pavement.
Ready for a pageant.
For one routine

quest for the ideal.
He's already seen
the rose itself
is not ideal.
He doesn't know
he's employed by a wraith

who gets her power
putting back the prickles,
reassembling the rose,
collecting all
the tacks discomforting to shoes
and inviolate skin

to make the rooted
creating rose itself
more comfortable,
able to deflect
the poor deer's nose,
the long stems of thorns

testing the nerve of true beauty.

Man with a Tail

anonymous snapshot found among antiques

In the garden our five-fingered hands
        seed and reap,
that birth bed of so many
        model vegetables,
caruncles still originate
on the odd tomato.

With people we take exception
        to the unplanned burgeon.
This young man's outdistances his spine.
        With dragonfly lightness,
slenderness, diaphaneity,
it points due south behind him,

and his glance back over his shoulder
        helps the shadowy visitor
to focus and forget himself
        and drop his fedora-
shaped shade in the foreground.
Its layer of touch cools the feet

of the fellow with the tail.
        The cauda is slim, straight,
proportional, and naked
        as is par for a gentleman
of this terrain, sodden and steep.
His immediate purview

is marked by sharp white switches
        taller than he and woven
in and out with others horizontally
        so as to suggest a palisade

of equal parts
protection and ventilation.

If there are spirits, they may
    pass through this residence of air
the temporal tribe constructs
    over metaphysical domain.
He knots a cord around his waist,
fixes in his hair a pillbox hat

of basketry—austere enough.
    But because of his excess,
he is never ancillary to anyone he knows
    or who has heard of his blest
nature consubstantiating kingdoms.
He could only feel balanced—

proud *and* humble, really—
    to have Creation written on him.
Down the Central Valley from me
    in a Lodi, California, pet shop,
a pearly oscar comes to light
with, on one fin, as discovered

by a Muslim customer, the "alif,"
    double "laum," and "ha,"
the word Allah,
    its calligraphic contrast
set there underwater as power
from an intimate far out in the universe

stirs the confining bowl of salty tropics
    and signs His name.
We thought we had a right
    to horror and disgust
based on a standard
of our fleshy selves,

but we're not prototypes.
    We might, in truth, want to restrain
God from creating, we who claim
    ecstatic pleasure in the zephyrous
cat's tail against our calves,
who swoon to the upbeat

of the mockingbird's fan. But think of us
    as glass. Think of us as rubbery—
à la kelp. Think of us as balsa. Model us,
    even now. If he were formed
of granite, an outcrop . . . Or if he were a comet
with his admired entitlement . . .

Think like God: Augment.
    This invention was so long
ago, and had almost seen oblivion
    except this science of images
leaves us his lizard electrons,
his sundial gnomon, his estate.

No one has ever seen it weary,
    no one has ever seen it old,
ever seen it fail, or ever fold
    and break. Extra. Like
desert-loomed camel tassels,
sopranino to our common altos,

added offspring to warm
    when it gets cold,
new track run for the pulse, beautiful
    living tablets of fish skin . . .
As time goes by, he is, I hope,
an ancestor, copying and copied.

Peppertree and Tea

in memoriam my birth father

The tires crush pepperberries
    when my sister and I arrive.
Seasoning, not gravel,
    beds the cottage drive:

all the songbirds have hot mouths,
    ants hotfoot through pink caves.
They are preferred burst bubbles,
    these radish pearls.

Where our old mystic father,
    that recondite cosmotheist,
used to step, in sandals, out to receive us,
    with cane, on door stone,

we splice forward,
    now through no one—
just through breathfuls
    of that spice.

Witherup writes:

    "Sipping mugs of blazing tea"

and

    "Two friends drinking tea in silence
    Is an image something like a rattlesnake
    Swallowing a meadowlark's egg—
    It may feed you for weeks."

Three-day widow says:

"Three days since the last tea."

Without the tea maker
at the understood hour—
afternoon's four—
nothing smells like tea
yet. The whole land's nippy
with pepperberries.
Trees spill pink purdahs
outside the flavored room
where he tasted new cigars.

A wash in the west sky
means one potful of rain.
Baskets, bags, boxes
of loose leaves. Today's choices—
jasmine, lychee, tit koom yum,
China black or China rose,
pan-toasted curves of an old, exacting,
inventive civilization,
often EverGreen.

Pots, strainers. One teaspoon
per cup? Without him
we can't remember. But that
turns out too strong.
Pour half down the sink.
Turn faucet into cup.
Not right. But just right.

To one outer bough
an Anna's hummingbird holds—
until a random sip
frees up

the evaporating bottom of the cup.
He lived in freedom
on dappled land, cabin in a bower,
office in a hut.

Not glum, too wired to the fates
of bird, mushroom, and time-telling tree,
the denizens of the property,
to be glum

except for urban greed's uprooting
of one and all. This is how I recall
him, who also loved
what I hardly had a chance to know he loved:

philosophy with coffee, a shrike in an oak.

Jeffrey Dahmer's Boots

Emmco, circa 1966, made in USA

Little red button
    tightening
the rim—
    clown
on toes, its head
    at stub-end
and feet sprawled
    up leg.
Elephant
    on heels.
Swags
    of a circus tent
decorate their wax red—
    a cinnamon
scented candle.
    A finger presses
into the run,
    overflow,
burning, pooling,
    round tallow edges like
the toes of these galoshes.
    They are in no way
rotted or decomposed
    or cracked or
split, no gravel
    stuck in the sole.
Our bodies
    are fretted,
stringy and pulpy,
    have too many textures
for simple childhood rubbers.

Our thoughts
drive at them like rain.
    His feet stay dry.
One almost looks
    for a wick
and a little flame.
    On these, the unmelted.

NOTE: Jeffrey Dahmer—serial killer, b. 1960 Milwaukee, Wisconsin; d. 1994
Columbia Correctional Institution, Portage, Wisconsin. The boots, on display in the
Cranbrook Academy of Art Museum, are from the collection of Harry Guild.

Chain

Twentieth-century-old Helen, a newborn bird,
was once in a room with Hitler
when, she said, his eyes were not entirely iced over,
his eyes were as yet early November,

leaf smoke such as made my eyes sting
when as a premature wife I walked the smoldering
gutters to our country library
for an afternoon with a book on Voodoo

from which I later used an image
—of a soul in a bottle—
in my first poem
about jealousy.

With the burning of time, only the Voodoo
has survived the *maitresse*
of a French Quarter museum
spellbinding in her cerulean

mail-order contact lenses—
not the least bit pitiless or absolute
but she can see the sky through me.
Jealousy led to simple tragedy

and it is now impossible to be in a room
with anyone who is not known
for destroying a life
as beautiful as spring or early autumn.

The look in their eyes can either be
naive and soft-hued
or soft-hued
and inhuman.

A Vigil, 2 A.M., County Jail

Waiting for their release—
for the shoes without laces,
the belts kept from suicide
—drumming, *When*
will they be released,
when and will they ever?
The hours so used
to their own sequence
cannot pass one another.
Diamond Ear waits here
for his *esposa,* and inside
the held-in selves stare
at their feet. They hate
the unbound, personal
tongues of their shoes.
Wives' eyes streetside
lynx on the transparent
jailhouse door. The stone
custodian entombs its men
in an infinite repeat of cells
like the guls in Persian rugs,
no escaping the eternal motifs,
the old, irresistible recurrences.
Will the stronghold
unbolt, will the men
spill out like rubble, gravel
at the foot of a weir,
will they sluice out, clean
and valuable again?

Then, in the darkest
hour out they pour,
their few clothes flying,
not birds migrating

into a pale limit of glass
but liquor wasting from
the crack in the punch bowl.
The women too, tough flutter
of shirt, not wings,
day legs tossed onto
cold night. The lost,
the drowned, and the plagued,
paroled in a bunch,
not sorted like washing
and eggs and nails.
And they don't all look so hurt
but glad to be loose
in their own t-shirts
to drift toward the bank
of chilly telephones.
Only one or two
get an embrace.
And I am chewed
by the serrated beauty
of a street tree, its raggedy
light-bronzed royalty
pinned in cement,
in its firm house
stationed to stretch out
as big as its life meant.

A Voyage with Patton

Patton's yacht, circling south from Hawaii,
with Patton's wife and young son,
a cook, and two other friends.
Based on the unpublished diary of James Wilder,
Sept. 11–Oct. 13, 1936

Not who you are but where
at noon, taking your sighting
of the floating sun, place
sliding out from under you
as it buoys your local company
who for this interval shares
vessel edges with you, no one
given more range than another,
the equilibrium of the boat.

Society—it is perfect in little,
a dish of appetizers, antipasto,
or *pupu* as they say in Hawaiian.
Some are here to learn to float
in darkness, some to train
their hands to guide and minds
to gauge, and one woman to
touch a child, one man more
to teach how to see the green.

'oma'oma'o? uliuli? mama'o?
Jade, Nile, silvergray, willow,
reed, frog, serpent, or spray?
So far it's just sea's indigo.
It shreds and knits, minces, mends.
But on verdure of light

the bookmarking of land depends.
An old copper impression of cloud
prints exactly atop the spot
where an atoll lolls.

Seven sailors anticipating,
and slighted by, signals from time,
that assiduous, throatless hum
beneath a cork pop
that releases one second
at a time. Are instants bottled,
floating in their own voyage?
For days no moment is named.
Time won't radio its sobriquet.

The Arcturus has its language though,
provincial with accents,
slaps, bangs, pitches, rolls.
The anchor chain rattles across coral
all night: an island's near.
Over moderate seas the schooner slides
and doesn't pound. In calms
it flops, just sits and wallows
while the sails flap, the booms
swing to and fro, and blocks
and tackles swash against the deck.
The squeak of deck shoes,
scuff of the diarist's pencil,
transpose the harmony on board.

The Colonel reckons the rank of wind.
If seamen gave wind deity,
just as well accredit it with rank.
All boulevard, say, and no byway.
A wind-road's racing stripes
sneak by the eyes. What strictly is it
that leads or draws, what signal, substance,

the nothing, really, that impels
when we sense it, surmise
the aura, the sanction, of a pilot?

They pass the island
without knowing. So now to double
back. Precariously from the foremast
hunt the vaporal green.
A fringe of coconut palms,
their quarry the clouds, and fading-in at once
Fanning Island washed turquoise
by the thrown light of the lagoon.

Then after music snagged from Salt Lake City
subbed for newscasts for a month,
a sudden bark of joy—"the time signal!"
Levenick has Mare Island on.
George had been just four seconds off.
His tabulations on the boat
were on the beat. At last
a broadcast, only to find that "nothing
startling has happened since we left."
They always had history,
concurrent with the day's affairs.

So they sail again.
Where? Where George showers
in fresh water of a squall.
Where? Somewhere among the
tuna, porpoises, the turbid schools.
Where? Where you can sleep
in rain, a rubber suit,
your rubber mattress oozing
like a sponge (sea or kitchen?)
with each roll of the yacht—
and not wake up.

Where? Where the chef cooks
just as well askew in squalls.
Where Georgie IV
salts his papaya. Where you have
to throw a spoiled jar of jellied
venison overboard. Where chowder's
made of sea-gleaned red snapper.
Where "there is nothing more rapid
than the sudden dash of a full
cup of coffee across the table."

> "After dinner we gathered on deck and everyone
> recited a poem. George was very good at it and
> rambled on far into the night. I never knew anybody
> who could remember so many."

And the poems were all martial,
Wilder said; nothing like Issa's

> From the bough
> floating down river,
> insect song.

Perhaps an ant war
but probably human, and, terribly,
mists of blood above the battlefield,
with few friends in insects
or song except

> *He, who had heard all day the Battle Hymn*
> *Sung on all sides by thousand throats of fire . . .*

Then

> *His early mind perverted by untruthful literature*
> *He sees a picture of war glorified . . .*
> *And knows not blood is pain and glory but a bubble . . .*

Muddied bubbles, he says in another. And

> *. . . in the subtle stillness after fight,*
> *In the half light between the night and day,*
> *We dragged his body, all besmeared with mud,*
> *And dropped it, clod-like, back into the clay.*

Hours later Wilder "took the wheel and although a bit cold
enjoyed sitting alone in the pouring rain,
singing all the songs I knew
at the top of my lungs."

> "Suddenly the sea became a mass of light. For a
> moment I was frightened thinking it might be the
> reflected lights of a passing ship." It lasted minutes,
> the phosphorus stirred by hidden swimmers
> to lit kindling.

Dodging coral heads to reach a wading foothold
on Palmyra, they are—who can say why?—
they *are* disappointed.
Piles of speckled eggs, hundreds
of red hermit crabs wandering among them,
coconuts, booby chicks ensconced in heliotrope shrubs.
Shark where Wilder was oozing
through a school of mullet, with eels.
He scares the shark with splashes.
Hosts of birdsnest ferns,
soft fine white coral sand lagoon-side;
oceanside, dirty brown and broken coral beaches.

The Colonel welcomed losing sight of land.
Those who didn't welcome it, he disdained.

People tell me these days
aren't important in Patton's life.
Didn't he know the importance
of a day? How to exact the location

of a day? How to be at peace
for weeks with six souls and a sea?
With himself? Things he'd respect,
gale and swell, ambitious
and impending, the dead calm and drizzle,
the uncaught idea-bodies of swerving fish.
And wasn't he at peace with shooting stars,
a sparrow blown out to sea,
the hygiene of brass and gear
and garments, the weather-scrubbed
body and the intelligence in order?

Peace without news
and the voyage finds its shore.
The incoming tureen
of people rocks a day
outside Pearl Harbor—
under quarantine.
Then they are covered in leis
and aloha like the welcomed
outcome to a light summer
mystery. Which was how, at sea,
they lullabyed victory
in its infancy.

NOTE: The Hawaiian words in stanza three mean, respectively, 'oma'oma'o, an
emerald; also name of a seaweed; uliuli, any dark color, including the deep blue of
the sea, the ordinary green of vegetation, and the dark of black clouds; mama'o,
greenish, light green. Issa wrote the haiku quoted above; the translators are Lucien
Stryk and Takashi Ikemoto. The lines from George S. Patton Jr.'s poems "A Soldier's
Burial," "Marching in Mexico," and "His early mind . . ." (from a 1905 letter to his
father) are included with the permission of Major General, Retired, George S. Patton.

A Perspective of Tangerines

When my birth father
   —as we knew him—
drew to his vanishing point,
   I hung a still life
by his painter friend,
   Michael
   Angelo,
on my birth mother's light-washed

cedar wainscot
   because she knew
the artist would call soon
   to pay his respects.
The painting pulsed best
   beneath an acrylic
   by my sister:
Fault-buckled, squirming,

feinting, upheaving,
   like Turkish
illuminated manuscript
   mountains, shapes
like ready fire-hose,
   wormy (she says)
   miles of coiling, stored
survival gear,

mountaineering
   (or deep-sea fishing)
ropes of colors—
   her family
of oranges and greens
   complemented

Mr. Angelo's
tangerines.

I hung his painting
   and stepped back.
Field of vision:
   citrus, Steinway,
morphine.
    Farther back,
   our father's
window's field:

valley oaks, nippy
   Peruvian pepper scent,
goats curiosity-proud,
   on a woodpile.
Watercress in late
   October creek,
   sun dusting itself
on sparrow

bathing-ground.
   And farther back:
whatever light
   and mist coalesce
with the verve
   of a traveling soul.
   In this way I could see
how perfectly placed he is.

III

Egypt at Sunset.
From My Window at Luxor.

Slowly very slowly the sun
Sinks to rest and none
Dare breathe. Even the breeze
Stirs hot. And like a frieze
Upon a wall the sun remains
For a moment and Africa reigns
Supreme. Now the Nile turns
From green to orange which burns
Its vivid way across all
The waters. The boatmen call
To one another. Their little crafts
Are black against the orange. Someone laughs
And it rings clear to the other side.
Now purple pink and gold appear wide,
Like a barrier across the sky.
The palm trees etched in black stand by
On guard. Like a spearhead in the night
The evening star appears. With its light
The twilight reign of Africa is broken.

      —I attribute this poem to Betty Offield. It was handwritten on
        half a sheet of paper folded and saved loose in the front of
        her diary of 1930, when she was 18–19.

At night in my room with the door closed
there was one voice that talked to me.
It sang on the wire in the late hours
and never gave up.
It was the mockingbird. I
had been saying my prayers as I knew
was right, had been begging and thanking.
I could feel my voice
though it said nothing aloud.
I could see despite the holy presences
my room remained dark.
But when the mockingbird sang
there was everything to be said, many melodies
to include. And through the rifts
in the curtains, green moonlight entered,
danced on my rumpled chenille.

Morticians from Duluth—who'd have thought
we'd spend vacation with them?
Camped in a body at Leech Lake,
they uncased their instruments,
played upbeat so we danced each night.
Their wives taller, wider than they,
playpens' corrals picketing the lakeshore,
they shared a crate of cheapest brandy.
I played along one time, on the electric piano
short on octaves, fragile diminutive highs
and groveling pitches in the depths.
I played along with happy undertakers.

Tri-Tactics

with a chorus from the rules of the British wartime board game

It is a government apartment
complex for the independent
insane and disabled, all of them
poor. The insane say it is just
for the poor and that they are
just poor. The insane woman's son
is slow-witted. She appears,
luckless and brainsick and thick,
one dusk on my porch.

There is no advantage in having the first move,
which is usually settled by lot,
and an attacker has no advantage
over the attacked.

She has threatened
the life of my daughter
but come here to tell me
she will protect my daughter
if I slow to her yellow light.
She thumbs eviction papers
making prose of the jeremiad
about her. The sun sags into smoke
from summer wildfires.
I pull her talk toward God,
she must leave fate to God,
not, herself, wreak it,
an undertaking like killing
a daughter. She says she steals
one of my potted plants and,
God knows, "What goes around
comes around," she will get hers.

An 'attack' is effected by a player moving a piece
onto a space next to an opponent's piece
so that the two are BACK TO BACK,
at the same time saying either 'Attack'
or 'No attack.' Attacking is optional.

> I stand up, it is time for her to go.
> You know after all how this war started?
> Outside the rules of the game.
> Outside at 5 A.M. on my daughter's patio,
> where she is fixing her bike.
> It's an hour when she feels peaceful.
> The tools are healing the bike and a car
> speeds round the corner and thumps
> against a cat and keeps on going.
> My daughter puts down her tools,
> goes out to the thrashing cat
> and carries it to the curb to comfort it
> through the dim hour in which it dies.

> This, in that neighborhood,
> is called seeing too much.

Searchlights are allowed a special move.
They may move any number of vacant spaces
but only to attack.

> And I turn on the porch lights
> so the woman ill in mind won't trip.
> Do you know what you've seen? I ask myself.
> Do you know what to do?
> Does she know what she's heard in my attention?
> Has the searchlight been converted
> to peacetime use? Do we believe
> it has no end, it just continues
> traveling out? Is there no conclusion
> to this game except Conscience?

64

It is our searchlight: If we think
it's dimming, is our only course of action
to let God dazzle us?

Ghazal: For My Students

A killdeer cries at night. Circular cries while flying. They say the
kindly Dalai Lama's voice is gruff. That he touches heads of people
in a queue for seven hours at a time. Two or three special things can
be said of anything and anybody. Of cat-beings, also, there are
virtues: they reach out an arm, they cry up, Sparky hoarsely, with a
tithe of a voice. I see the poets begging, and not with a bowl of song:
begging with an empty bowl of fame. Do they not know winter's
complete, available gray? Birch wands wax a stripped yellow, broken
eggshell, weed-ivory, field-of-cornhusk. The frozen ground-flowers'
leaves lapse over to show their coin-silver lining. Don't be personally
famous. When you pray, get down on a million knees.

Seven Telegrams to Miss Olive M. Richards

found among antiques

Olive's mother sings.
She wants her daughter
to hear vibrato
through the telegram.
But it isn't the singing kind—
that's not invented yet.
It doesn't even allow breath a phrase,
all upper case,
no dotted cues, dashed prompts, in sight.
But it shows standing,
in loud and pressing intonation.

From San Francisco, September 15, 1924:
GLAD YOU ARRIVED SAFE HOPE YOU LIKE
NEW YORK REGARDS TO MR SAMOILOFF MA
IS KEEPING FINE SANG FOR MRS CAREY BIG
SUCCESS WILL SEND MONEY SHORTLY PETS
ARE ALL WELL BEST REGARDS AND LOVE
TO LOUIS LOVE MOTHER

Seven skits of suspense.
In each Miss Olive is adored, fussed
over, coddled, keenly missed,
suspected, promised a kiss.
All transmissions say
YOU DON'T WRITE ME ENOUGH.
Where *did* so many letters go astray,
flown but still to perch,
myriad sent (or merely meant)?

My daughter plays Morse alphabet
for me over the phone. PHOEBE

. _ _ .   . . . .   _ _ _   .   _ . . .   .
and the word SHIT   . . .   .   _
she likes in code-stretched cadence.
She's boning up to take
a ham test where she'll need
to tap and hear, pure hand and ear,
five words per minute. She aspires
to fill and empty twenty.

"If a high tension condenser is connected across the spark gap,
the spark shortens and thickens, turns bluish white. The sound of
the spark increases to a crash . . ."

From San Francisco, September 25, 1924:
CANNOT UNDERSTAND NO MAIL FROM US SENT
LETTER DAILY FORGET YOUR HOMESICKNESS MA
WANTS YOU TO STUDY HARD DID YOU GET THE
FIFTY WE GOT VERY DISCOURAGING LETTERS
FROM LOUIS SAYING YOU ARE HOMESICK DO
NOT ALLOW ANYTHING TO INTERFERE WITH
YOUR CAREER MA IS FINE LOVE DAD

Who's to say it wasn't electricity she conducted: Autistic, my
daughter used to tap, tap on a thing to learn its substance, not grip it
close, but know it from a test of pat and brush and tap.

From Albany, New York, October 6, 1924:
HELLO SWEETHEART GOSH I MISS YOU WISH
YOU WERE HERE HAD BLUES ALL DAY SHOW
FINANCIAL SUCCESS PERFORMANCE TERRIBLE
TWO NEW PEOPLE IN PARIS TONIGHT REHEARSED
ALL DAY TOMORROW TEN THIRTY WROTE LAST
NIGHT WILL WRITE TONIGHT AWFULLY TIRED
THINK OF YOU ALWAYS LOVE AND KISSES
REGARDS TO ALL LOUIE

Today, priced to move, two dollars per telegram, whatever use
they are to you. The vendor peddles old theater costumes too. Vel-

vets, braids, Elizabethan. He's spread his wares on a dusty lot, foot of a gold town's cobbled main street. It begins to rain. Tea-yellow and crackly, burnt brown on the folds and smelling of decay of sachet, the telegrams will make you worry—why *do* you want them?

"If now the key is depressed, a spark should pass across the spark gap unless this gap is too long."

From Albany, October 7, 1924:
HELLO SWEETHEART YOU MUST HAVE
FORGOTTEN ME ONLY RECEIVED ONE WIRE
AND NO LETTERS SO FAR SHOULD YOU CARE
TO WASTE FIFTEEN MINUTES WRITE CARE
WORCESTER THEATER WORCESTER MASS MAY
NOT WRITE TONIGHT BELIEVE YOU COULD
HAVE FOUND FIFTEEN MINUTES TO WRITE
EITHER SUNDAY OR MONDAY LOVE AND
KISSES LOUIE

Phoebe got 100% on her telegraphy test.
One week later another operator slashed her tires.

What is your distance?
What is your true bearing?
Where are you bound for?
How many words have you to send?

I am receiving badly.
I am being interfered with.
Atmospherics are very strong.
Increase power.
Send slower.
I have nothing for you.

Shall I stand by?

From Albany, October 8, 1924:
HELLO HONEY GETTING READY TO LEAVE

FOR WORCESTER UNABLE TO WRITE TONIGHT
AS WE ARE MAKING JUMP RIGHT AWAY HAVE
HAD BLUES FOR FOUR DAYS WILL BE TICKLED
WHEN I GET HOME AGAIN TO YOU WRITE OR
WIRE CARE FIREBRAND COMPANY WORCESTER
THEATER HOPE YOU ARE WELL LOVE KISSES
REGARDS LOUIE

"In contrast to the thin feeble discharge at the secondary, usually obtained, this electrolytic interruptor transforms the spark into a flaming caterpillar . . ."

Does the widow hear from her beloved,
as years of separation wear away,
as much as when he'd just passed on?
He used to find her keys, feel warm
on doorknobs, occupy the body
of her recollection. No intercession
but frank touch signaling, nudging,
steering flesh with spirit firsthand.

From Worcester, Massachusetts, October 9, 1924:
SOMETHING WRONG NO WORD TODAY
ANSWER MY EXPENSE NECESSARY LOVE LOUIE

Brief Chinese love poems/letter poems/loss poems take gaudier and wrigglier images into their arms. Would a wire welcome amber waters of a canal, hair too short to hold a hairpin, a girl with a green skirt on sloped grass, a wine cloud, boiling water, crinkled red petals, a herdsman's horn? Would it unveil this way: "my eyes/go out/to the end/of every/incoming/road."

From Worcester, October 10, 1924:
DEAREST SWEETHEART FORGIVE MY HASTE BUT
HOW COULD YOU FEEL IF YOU HAD NOT
RECEIVED LETTER FROM ME YOU CAN IMAGINE
HOW YOU FELT WHEN YOU DIDN'T HEAR FROM
ME FROM LOS ANGELES MIGHT LEAVE TWO AM

SUNDAY ARRIVE EIGHT WILL LET YOU KNOW
LOVE AND KISSES LOUIE

And completely *without* desperate love, with love, instead, of solitude and old age, while a westerly tosses pear boughs in a mountain garden and boys come to steal fruit—send a telegram like that. Or like the poem in early summer about the gentle sot riding a brown cow, *and* a recipe included in the same thirty-seven English words: "Cut chives/salt leeks/corn/to make a paste . . ." Wouldn't you return code after code of love to such a correspondent?

"Messages should be fun,"
said George Oslin
in 1933 against the grain.
How could he convince us?—
Lucille Lipps sang the first musical
telegram to ridicule.
Long lived Mr. Oslin,
to ninety-seven,
distinguished by the melody
of his messagery.

It is all pointillistic—our piecemeal testimonials, bit-by-bit depositions of affection, so much we're missing, saying, missing, saying—pointillism and shed eyelashes.

But the fitful pieces work,
they spark, they speak.
Heard, they're held.
And now they're ours,
our flock of intimations
shepherded in search
of one that's absent,
we fear distracted,
through the dark.

NOTE: Quoted portions are based on statements from the *Manual of Wireless Telegraphy*, Leo J. Meyberg Co., San Francisco, undated. Chinese translations are from *Old Friend From Far Away*, North Point Press, San Francisco, 1980.

Last October

We took flashlights among the dead white birds and to the white terrain of their droppings. The webs of spiders seemed mild. The handheld light beam works like a feather, so there was a sense of oversize flurry as we walked back through the warehouse. Haunting colors, the browns, grays, darks, and straight leaks of day like ruled lines in early geometric abstract paintings. I brought home a watercolor the other day by a woman who laid a tile floor in her sunroom to look like waterlilies and a pool. She finished it and two days later died. Her painting partner said they painted the sheep outside a barn together from a photograph. "Genevieve liked pink," she said. I'd picked up the scene for the pastels in the barn. On the dawn way to Galt, fog up to the knees, to the backbones, of cattle. Then the sun comes up, takes the fog in its mouth.

Given and Received

When April's
grape tendrils
tackle our small
St. Francis,

they knock him over
when they only
hope to use him
as a brace.

I find such undoing
hard to face.
Should I
see the tendril

laughable
for what it's done,
toying with
a holier, heavier

avatar and messing up?
All I did
was love,
there's not a one of us

can't say,
and a saint landed
on his back,
gazed up

through
determination
in the guise
of wine's leaves

and lay perfectly
unable to rise.
All I do is love,
the profuse fuss

of the garden swears.
Another year,
a snail climbed
that adamant goodness

to rest out
April storms
in tolerant,
durable arms.

Dear Diary, Betty Offield, 1925

There *is* a world of lemonade and swans,
the young girls resting out the heat on lawns
beside Parisian water and its ferrying skiffs.
They have been out dancing and they're
only thirteen. They were, of course,
politely, firmly told to stop, in Paris,
in public, two girls *are not allowed to dance
together* even if they're both named Betty.
Even if on other days they play
Duck on a Rock, want dolls for a birthday,
take goat rides down the Champs Élysées.
You need to understand girls
who understand a beautiful life
with the depth of Rembrandt's
conversancy with darkness, how
it is really mixed into a climactic mist
on the shimmering moon's palette of eclipse.

Betty draws and paints too. Shelled
French village homes make awful lace,
look like Pompeii. Near Villa D'Este
a view *looks just like Catalina,*
which her family owns. (On
Catalina, a boulder in the sun appears
as though it had glass spears through it.)
Horses with suits of silver. Venetian lanterns.
A funeral procession in Verona carries voices
of so many children, she gathers the dead's
a girl. In Belgian battlefields *the trenches
are full of water and the trees nothing
but stumps.* A man with palsy treads
in wooden shoes. These subjects serve
in place of school though she loves her teacher
in America with a galvanizing crush,

and without blush, enrapturing *Dear Diary*
with how beautiful is divine Miss Bell,
every scolding word coming from her mouth
she adores, can't bear to miss her when Miss
Bell is ill, so delivers her a concert ticket
as pretext to see *my darling* open her door.
She knows she's overblazing but trusts
this watermarked confessor, this linen page.

With girlfriends she plays cards without
her clothes, until a rap from the delivery man.
But likes clothes too: those bridesmaids
dressed in pink, with brown straw hats,
bunching roses on the side, pink satin bags
with orchids and ferns. And there are
other colors: *In the afternoon,*
we saw a dead man, killed in a taxi,
his face was purple and smashed in.

Out of a letter from Elsa Armour II
slips a news shot of Betty's grandparents,
Wrigleys—*thought you'd want to know.*
Under spring trees, with the Kellogg Betty
and an unsmiling English girl—*predictably!*—
she's reading *Dracula.* Caught in
their own spell, they pick the hotel
flowers, buy lavender ribbon in Evian,
make bouquets to give their moms
about to leave them with a governess
who teaches leather crafts.
Betty beats Betty at tennis.
They're noticed by *The Prince.*
He asked if we wanted to go for a walk.
It was only about 8:30 and not dark
so we went. We went through woods
two or three miles. I thought we would never
get home. He kept taking my hands
and Betty's. I walked ahead, left him with her.

(I try to scan his exiled Russian autograph.
All its many names are of another world
and that world's hand.)

The night Betty Offield turns fourteen,
she watches mounted Cossacks
jump through flame. Another night,
*a naughty play where none of the women
wore any clothes.* She sizes up, in one
chateau they tour, *the skeleton
of the famous race horse Flying Fox*
and *great big stones from horses' stomachs.*
She weighs 88 pounds dressed, with chocolate
an almost daily inner beauty regimen.

There's nothing frantic or zany in her voice.
Consummately without guilt or defiance
of the testy kind. No sense of failing
at anything. Nor stress to prove herself
resplendent with success. Guided through
dungeons, she doesn't know she didn't learn,
in Miss Harris's school in Illinois, how to spell
torchur.

Last week she visited
the house where Dante lived when he was a poet.
On a lone page without a date—it's oddly
the book's first leaf and not the last—
she floats a summary:

*Orange blossoms picked at Sorrento.
Laurel leaves at Pompeii.
The candle given at the Catacombs.
The lava (black) saved from Vesuvius.
Sulphur discovered at Little Vesuvius.
Statue of St. Francis, at the church, Assisi.
Sea shells: the Lido.*

The bay leaves from Pompeii
still prickle between blank pages.
I try to woo back their cool aroma but it's gone.
That's why we need her words, how at the Doge's palace
We saw the largest picture in the world, of Paradise.

Philosophy

from the journal of Betty Offield, age 18, 1930

We got out of the taxi. It was a perfectly black street.
Suddenly from nowhere five women appeared.
One was my size, had a boyish bob and a trench coat.
She said Bon soir *and so did I.*
Then she walked up to me and squeezed my arm so it hurt!
I came over to Russell. All the girls laughed.
She kept bumping up against me then.
I was so scared.
We walked away and two of them had a necking party
then disappeared. Don't know whether they were men
dressed as women for White Slave trade or—fairies!

It's like a drug that gets hold of me—a pursuit of a good time . . .

Malaga. At the Spanish lesson she's arranged:
The old man, stunning looking, with his valet,
was in the Titanic disaster. He got in a lifeboat
either dressed in women's clothes or not—
his wife kept yelling at him not to let others
in so he pushed people's hands off the boat.
That was twenty years ago and he is still
kicked out of all the clubs in England.
People recognize him and hate him.
And he is so so sweet. His name is
Sir Don Gordon.

Life seems to be just a bubble—a lovely shiny bubble . . .

Mlle terribly drunk.
She and the Spaniard necking. It was awful.
They were shooting rats downstairs with pistols!

Then Mlle started crying!

That's life—happiness mixed I guess . . .

Two carloads of girls from her finishing school,
touring Delft, pile out to inspect a Protestant church:
Too awful.
Whitewashed, no altar, no decoration.
Supposed to concentrate on God only.
Atrocious thing.

The drug wears away. Like a dope fiend I suffer from its after
effects . . .

Then to Ghent, to church of St. B_____.
Service so we had to pray.
Man with spear told us to be quiet!
Holy Blood here.
A drop of Christ's Blood, in a tube.
They have processions & carry it . . .

. . . right in your grasp—
you reach for it—it suddenly bursts at your touch
and the soap stings your eyes . . .

What is philosophy's first cry? First step?
On what does it nurse? What toys does it take up,
outgrow? What can it hand down
to the next-in-need? On what blackboard
does its wisdom not press off into dust?
Is this it?—Life is terribly odd things paired
with clichés? Can truth's lyrics
lack harmonics? Mustn't
the great questions sing? Sing
into the starved acoustics
of abject alcoves, vacant niches,
warble fundamentals

into indigence of insipid channels,
airless cul-de-sacs, scuffed streets,
drained fountains—sanctuaries—
when you find their echo-places?
This girl is only eighteen.
Her marrow grows. Be sure,
the drop of lamb's blood
parades its ongoing fatality.
Millions live by its philosophy.
But there are other ones.
She watches the sky
in pleasure boats' waters
she could mix with that stain.
I think it's dawned on her
that they always reflect,
that nothing can stop
their flow of reflection day and night . . .

Principles

"Temporary Models" for the Donkey went out to animators—with injunctions: "Note ragged hairline and mane," and "Always carry a doleful expression on faces unless extremes call for the contrary." It is a secret: "Basically, Mickey is *still* a pear-shaped character." His "ears are *not circles*." His arms "slide off the shoulders." Keep his "hands fairly large and full." "There is a feeling of flatness" enters a life, or it's just a detail of Mickey's sniffer. Being: a composition of expressive principles. Myth: the same. Real work is making the Goof slouch, and one eyelid slightly slouchier than the other and the little round tum-tum not global but like a paint blister on the sunny side of a house. No shadow on the flirty dog unless she's very close. She bats an eye.

My cartoon of principles: a flat valley, a bulbous hill—a principled place. A tree of will, a creek of change. And the good sense, & senses, to recognize it as one's home. An animal haven with beings bright-eyed, tickled pink, fired up, propelled. I'll be caught talking to my tenets and codes, golden rules of thumb, for I lived so long in silence, in a numb humor, in the unprincipled.

Material Theology

Mennonite quilt, 1890-1910, Pennsylvania

In Exodus: *They are to make the ephod of gold, purple stuffs, violet shade and red, crimson stuffs, and fine twined linen, the work of a skilled embroiderer. And for Aaron's sons you shall make coats and sashes and caps; you shall make them for glory and beauty.*

For Ohio Amish the *ordnung: No ornamental, bright, showy, form-fitting, immodest or silk-like clothing of any kind. Colors such as bright red, orange, yellow, and pink are not allowed. Clothing in every way modest, serviceable, and so simple as scrupulously possible.*

In Kansas: *Mennonites raised flax and hemp and sheep for wool. The thread for weaving was sometimes taken to a non-Mennonite weaver. The colors were usually monochrome, the favorites blue, black, or brown.*

We stood in the big barn
buying someone else's theology:
the dealers specialized
in bedding obedient to the sweep
of pasture and barn light and faith,

and we knew what beliefs
we could ask for and which
must go on being with God
and without us,
their credo and canon of color

go on appropriate to God's
underslip and coat lining.
There were no diaries but these
of the revelatory winds

through the principled settlements
in those stretches.
When it reached my home,
I could no longer see it.
My eyes monochromed,
their God didn't radiate here.

I looked and looked.
A season changed,
and I invited light again.
Plush!—why it's like my cat's eyes when I can't see their colors, their
change when he comes in at different times of day. In one light I see
a fern pattern in the velvet. It speaks of God as moss does on dirt or
bark. God approves the bruno, the velvet brick, the iron clay, the
furrow's plough-shaving.

In the Plains: *Beauty was so absent from early pioneers' daily lives
that they rejoiced when they discovered some. Jacob Schmidt, a Rus-
sian Mennonite immigrant, made a note in his diary on April 19,
1875: 'Found a little white flower today.'*

How do you tell religious darkness from religious light?
For the drab, Christ crucified is lumber business.

Theological darkness
is believing in a god more absent than dim.
The student asking, "What's an insight?"

In Canada:
*Some destructive tendencies
one finds among Mennonites:
rigidity, pressure to conform,
lack of self-acceptance,
being self-critical,
avoidance of emotional issues.
There occasionally is mention
of depression as the 'Mennonite disease.'*

Try to show an image of the structure of the deiform, the design of the godly, look inward first, say brown is your favorite pigment of nature. You can start with the brown sloped sides of cinnamon goats and kine. Stars sometimes imagine themselves in neat rows like children on the first day of school. All this is agreeable to a God that you find shining on your household and deep brown farm on the best of days.

S tells me: "My mother fainted—it was my new dress,
it went against her theology
for me to wear to church, sleeves
to the wrist, round high neckline,
hand-woven, straight shape
skipping the waist, what's to fear?
—It was orange."

In Pennsylvania: *The Religious Society of Friends believes an Inner Light, God's spirit, lies within each person and through that Light religious truth is known. All people are equal as they all possess the Inner Light. Material possessions sustain equality, peace, community, and simplicity by avoiding excesses of worth or quantity. Plainness of speech and dress avoids concerns that could obstruct the Light.*

In Proverbs:
*Like apples of gold in a silver setting
   is a word that is aptly spoken.
A golden ring, an ornament of finest gold,
   is a wise rebuke to an attentive ear.*

This quilt reifies
divine watchfulness, peerlessness, immanence.

God
has
fiber.

In Samuel:
O daughters of Israel, weep for Saul
who clothed you in scarlet and fine linen,
who set brooches of gold
on your garments.

In Peter: *Let not yours be the outward adorning with braiding of the*
hair, decoration of gold, and wearing of robes, but let it be the hid-
den person of the heart . . .

Rays keep sallying forth from the seated schoolroom stars
and they are a deep wine-brown, shaded plum-
mustard, green of the creek in a dense coastal canyon,
charcoal of the hearth bricks, and a horse-velvet brown.

In Isaiah: *That day the Lord will take away the ankle ornaments,*
tiaras, pendants and bracelets, the veils, headbands, foot chains and
belts, the scent bottles and amulets, signet rings and nose rings, the
expensive dresses, mantles, cloaks and purses, the mirrors, linen gar-
ments, turbans and mantillas.

But when he's through this is a God who will gaze out of many lights.
He has a conscience of colors.
His comparisons are so deep and brilliant they make you squint.
He can bundle up
the cold air separating you from him.
He is a solid color God
and of fine quality,
dusky mohair and outward-shining rose wool,
he is matte and plush, tenebrous and kindled.
He is lasting and contrasting.

Hawaiian Buddha

Slow down.
        —Lowell Fulson

How is it lived in,

mortals' ideal atoll
where the immortal, in order
    not to appear as dead,
    has come to life in wood?

If you are the image of insight—
eye-level knees, ox-shouldered,
    widebreasted Buddha—
    how can we too be burly?

I place at your feet an offering
of noticing, which is not
    enlightenment. You
    glance down

with a limit of your own:
you're seated but not enthroned.
    There are other steps
    and stepless places

to surrender shoes;
and while there are other Buddhas
    who follow the curve
    of the heated sea

until it cools on shores
of more ascetic supplicants,
    though not more naked,
    only you know

the soul growls
in its fat sculpture,
    starved for too much.
    The mad devotee

pins herself
in the hair of flowers.
    How small
    is the smallest thing

that wants to engulf everything?

Byodo-in Temple

At John's

Watching Walter at John's Barber Shop, I decided I couldn't bear my snaggy weight of hair. Of the three barbers, the woman would do a woman. Terry sprayed a mist unlike any exact flower at my head and said she liked the color. That's my real color. I know, she said. My mother's long white hair, I began, when I first met her . . . She interrupts, Are you adopted? She is. Wonders if she should not meet her father. But that isn't her story—she said she got pregnant out of wedlock. I did too. She arranged an adoption through her family doctor. Later she searched for her son. They told her of his suicide when he was twenty. I wasn't in any room or any chair. I was entering her eyes as a plane flies into a vast cloud and sees no other realm. Her face became a hard-earned gem place with no hinged welcome, and some call that glorious. We suffer when we have preferences, when we prefer that life not be like that. A mineral has made a decision, no, taken a step, no, gotten old, no, been oppressed, I should think so, thought blue, thought clear, let it proceed. I can't remember who I've been with in caves because a cave is a crystal place and you wear your warm things there. Concentrate on what's for the best. Feathers and wool . . . I once had a coat made of bat wings. A slicker. If you see bats without their own glove hide on, you see they are delicate hands. Five fingers' bones are what a bat wing is. A bat is a small body piloted by two enormous hands. By gloves. Dusk is their time of wonder. And if we must have war, rubble, fires, there is lots of room to fly over our desolation.

Gypsy Life

Each summer before
I came to be very sure,
I listened to possibilities
from the steady sentencing hands
of the automated gypsy.
Lovely in beads,
gold and black,
and a long-lasting rose,
she couldn't breathe,
sealed inside a booth,
anything but cards of prophecy.
Her fortunes only cost a penny.
Soon I had a life plan.
When I thought Grandmother
would like to know
how I turned out
(a preview),
I let her read
the half-dollar deck.
She was, in her shawl,
a gypsy the dusk made gray.
"I've had
all those fortunes," she'd say.

Driving in Circles with the Blind

I have enough retablos of visions, ex-votos of rescues,
for a shrine in a corner of my home
to pray for release from the mind's mad portraitist—
Wendy's sick green angel of the asylum,
William's fisherman curled up
in his own tackle box, Alice's hunched figure outlined
with scraping fingernail through blue gouache.

I've seen how lunacy spells people, hello
in a möbius monologue, a post-tribulationist
vaudeville act of God. One night when I was about
to furl into sleep and fathom some new low
dream of fear (blind cave cricket dream
would do it), not knowing whether by morning
jangles would be re-wound, or backbone built,

I heard a knock at the door, I rose from bed,
and hesitated until the rap said who it was,
then I unlocked all brass latches to the night
and my own flesh and blood.
A long white limousine blinded the street.
But who does she know who owns *anything*?
They pooled and rented it because

I was the mother her friends wanted to meet.
The door to it stood wide and, inside,
two strange faces phosphoresced—
from some cold arson of the mind?
Even though they could not see me,
they implored me to ride with them.
I left home barefoot, bowed into the limousine.

The driver began to move us swiftly over the ground.
One rider's name was Ronnie. He called the young woman ÕÓOs.

Os is not her real name. Os is her simple name,
oneness, oddness, own-ness.
Os is her owl name, her night name.
She desires OOOOOOOO
small circles. Can she feel this large one,

this tire-tread round of miles we begin?
She has a circular face
and pretty, dark corkscrews of curls.
She craves circles drawn in the foundling-skin
palm of her hand—a wispy, sprouted wand
pruned for use in pagan ceremony. She rubs
the round bevel of the watch crystal on my wrist.

A *hoop*, a *loop*, a *noose*, they're all her thing.
Then she slides forward, drops to her knees
in front of me, her arms encircle my waist,
she calls it *Mother*, she names it *Sis*.
Ronnie, everyone knows, will speechify
full speed, filibuster all he understands
is missing. Neither he nor Os

can walk. Anymore. They both love wheels
and feel them fasten on like flesh.
They want to take their wheelchairs to
Hawaii and my daughter to fix them.
But we are just circling a dark school,
Ralph Waldo Emerson Junior High,
owl-calls over its empty track, the invisible

percussion of its tennis courts, its uncheering
football fields. We are driving around the dark
estate of public knowledge.
In our mobile asylum
one echolalic delights another, lingers
in the shell of mimic music,
appeals to me to impersonate them both.

The more we say what each other says,
the more we vow we're different.
But aren't we all—or aren't *they*, at least—
God's creatures? God's creatures know
the OOOÖÖ**OOOO**ōõõ**OOOO**
*ooooo*ÔÔÔÔÒÒÒÒÒ*oo* õ͂õ͂õ͂õ͂
OOOOØØØØ☺☺☺☺

☻☻☻☻ **OOOO** ∞∞∞∞∞∞∞
◻◻◻◻◻◻◻◻◻◻◻◻◻◻◻◻◻◻◻◻◻◻
ₒₒₒₒ°°°°°°°OOOOO
OOOO **òòòòòòòøø %‰%‰%‰%‰**
oo, all the Os that open up the night sky
(in or out of the mind)
and pattern it with awe.

So far I can ask the coachman
to slow to a stop, if I choose; I can open the door
to re-enter the world solid as a consonant.
But God's creatures put their spin
on it. And life by life
God's brood is lifted out where each one rents,
the point on the arc, the warp on the bend.

May each have an oasis. A moat. A moon phasing in.
A mother in mind. Release.
May each have a prayer, even if on waking
they go out to touch their dream's circumference
and find it too mean but at least real,
a wheelbarrow, a roller skate, a shopping cart,
a one-speed bike, on the sidewalk, at the curb,

ready to go forward, idling, a little way . . .

ABOUT THE AUTHOR

Raised in California, Sandra McPherson received her B.A. at San Jose University and studied at the graduate level with Elizabeth Bishop and David Wagoner at the University of Washington. Her poetry collections include *Edge Effect* (Wesleyan University Press, 1996), *The Spaces Between Birds* (Wesleyan University Press, 1996), *The God of Indeterminacy* (University of Illinois Press, 1993), and *The Year of Our Birth* (Ecco, 1978), which was a finalist for the National Book Award. Her other collections are *Streamers* (Ecco, 1988), *Patron Happiness* (Ecco, 1983), *Radiation* (Ecco, 1973), and *Elegies for the Hot Season* (Indiana University Press, 1970); reprinted by Ecco, 1982). Her honors include two grants from the Ingram Merrill Foundation, three National Endowment for the Arts fellowships, a Guggenheim Foundation Fellowship, and an award in literature from the American Academy and Institute of Arts and Letters. She taught for four years at the Iowa Writers' Workshop, and has been on the teaching staff of many writers' conferences, including the Geraldine R. Dodge Poetry Festival, and the Art of the Wild. Her poetry was also featured in the PBS special "The Language of Life," hosted by Bill Moyers. She is Professor of English at the University of California at Davis. She is founder, editor, and publisher of Swan Scythe Press.